Menus and Music

Menus and Music

MENU COOKBOOK
WITH MUSIC FOR DINNER AND DESSERT

by

Sharon O'Connor

Menus and Music Productions, Inc.
Berkeley, California

Library of Congress Cataloging in Publication Data
O'Connor, Sharon. 1948–
Menus and Music ™
A Menu Cookbook with a Musical Cassette for Dinner and Dessert
with Music by The San Francisco String Quartet

Includes index
1. Cookery   2. Entertaining
I. Title
85-90435
ISBN 0-9615150-0-7 (pbk.)

Menus and Music ™ is published by

Menus and Music Productions, Inc.
3303 Dwight Way
Berkeley, CA 94704
(415) 845-6614

Book and cover design by Sharon Smith Design
Cover photograph by Jim Sadlon
Food styling by Sharon Polster
Violin and bow from the collection of Joseph Gold
Composition by Ann Flanagan Typography

Manufactured in the United States of America

10 9 8 7 6 5 4 3 2

*To my husband, John, and our two children
Claire and Caitlin*

CONTENTS

DESSERTS

COCOLAT
Schön Rosmarin   87

JUST DESSERTS
Rondeau   91

LA VIENNOISE
Linzertorte   95

SHERATON-PALACE HOTEL
Garden Court Trifle Bowl   97

ACKNOWLEDGMENTS

I would like to thank the many people who contributed to this project.

To Nathan Rubin, James Shallenberger, and David George, fellow members of the San Francisco String Quartet.

To the chefs who contributed menus and recipes to the cookbook. These include Alice Waters, Fritz Streiff, Judith Ets-Hokin, Judy and Norman Sawicki, Sharon Polster, Ted Smith, Betsy Ayers, Marty Rosenblum, Brian Leonard, Alice Medrich, Karen Shapiro, and Jane Fay. I would also like to thank Robin McMillan, Timothy Maxson, Donna Balsamo, Nancy Van Wyk, Barbara Radcliffe, and Elliot Hoffman, who own and manage the catering and dessert companies.

I want to especially thank Thomas DeAngelo for his continuing support during the past ten years at the Sheraton-Palace Hotel.

To David Porter, who engineered the cassette at the Music Annex Recording Studios.

To my editor, Carolyn Miller, for being so flexible and thorough.

To Sharon Smith for her wonderful design and her support of this project.

To my friend Joseph Gold, whose violin and bow appear on the cover.

My sincere thanks to Sharon Polster of Edible Art for her food styling, Jim Sadlon for his photograph, and Merilyn Moss for the calligraphy.

To Martha Rubin for her help in producing the cassette and for her moral support throughout this entire project.

To John Coreris for his help with the conception and production of this project.

To all the people who have enjoyed the music of the San Francisco String Quartet.

To my mother and father for all those music lessons and for instilling in me the love of beauty.

And thanks again to John, Claire, and Caitlin for putting up with me during all this work.

INTRODUCTION

The two loves of my life are great music and great food—and I think they are inseparable! I have been interested in combining these two arts ever since I graduated from the University of California at Berkeley and went for more study at the Music Conservatory in Amsterdam. Besides studying music in Amsterdam, I also learned a great deal about good food as I traveled through Europe. I came back to California with a decision to shape my life around music and food.

In 1975 I founded the San Francisco String Quartet, and we began performing dinner music in the Sheraton-Palace Hotel's Garden Court, which has been called "the most beautiful dining room in the world." The quartet has been giving weekly performances in the Garden Court for the past ten years now, as well as presenting concerts in traditional halls. Over the years we have also been frequently asked to perform for elegant private and corporate dinner parties. Our repertoire on these occasions consists of quartets by composers from Bach to Debussy, intermingled with shorter works. We have been nurturing a love of chamber music while people nourish themselves!

We have kept our standards the same whether we are playing background dinner music or a concert in a hall. In fact, classical music was not always meant to be performed only in concert halls—composers wrote for opera houses, and also for dining rooms, parlors, and gardens. Mozart wrote his serenades, cassations, divertimenti, and *notturni* for these places, and Telemann, inventing an even more specific genre, wrote his "Table Music." Before 1800, composers showed no disinclination to serve prosaic needs (or to hear their works accompanied by the sounds of conversations, or of knives and forks). Nor did they let such needs limit their craft—the music has survived for more than two centuries.

Anyone who has ever experienced the art of fine dining will probably remember that moment throughout his or her life. The music performed during the dining experience makes that moment even richer. The pieces included on the musical cassette accompanying this book will make a dinner stand out in your memory of fine dining.

I was prompted to undertake this project because I have been performing dinner music for the past ten years, yet every time I gave my own dinner parties I had a difficult time finding appropriate music. I would finish my kitchen preparations, check the living and dining rooms, and then go change. My guests would usually be arriving by the time I thought to find the music that would accompany the evening. The radio had disrupting commercials, and my record and cassette collection did not seem to include music that was really geared to be dinner music.

In planning this book and tape, I have made sure that all of the menus from the cookbook are perfectly accompanied by the music presented on the cassette. I chose as contributors to the cookbook chefs who have presented food for the most lavish occasions in the San Francisco Bay Area at which the San Francisco String Quartet has also performed. I also gave the contributing chefs a preliminary tape of pieces that were to be included on the cassette so they could listen to the music before creating the menus and recipes for this project. Alice Medrich from Cocolat was inspired to create a new dessert named after one of the musical selections on the dessert side of the tape, "Schön Rosmarin." The chefs from Chez Panisse, Taste, and Just Desserts also gave musical names to their creations.

I don't think there are any hard and fast rules for dinner music except that the music should never be too strident or exciting, since this might stir up some adrenalin, which hinders the flow of digestive juices. At the beginning of an evening, our quartet usually performs up-tempo Baroque or Classical pieces in a major key that stimulate and brighten spirits and invite people in. The dinner music is chosen to give a feeling of warmth and comfort, and the dessert music is light and sweet-sounding. After dinner we choose pieces that are reflective and have a feeling of repose and contentment. The music unifies the evening and evokes a sequence of feelings.

Music for a dinner can be chosen for a variety of reasons. Whimsy enters in when we perform Saint-Saëns's "The Swan" at the Fairmont Hotel while waiters carry candelit ice-carved swans around the room for the serving of the *sorbet*. It seems humorous to perform only pieces that are in compound time and that accumulate interest at elegant dinners for bankers. Sometimes we make certain musical selections because they seem very appropriate, such as when we performed Bach's "Jesu Joy of Man's Desiring" at a luncheon for Cardinal Casserole after the opening of the Vatican Collection at the de Young Museum. We have performed Vivaldi's "Spring" from his *Four Seasons* for a spring dinner such as the one presented on page 49, and we played only Mozart quartets for a dinner after the first private screening of the movie *Amadeus* in San Francisco. Music is often chosen for romantic reasons. We were once asked by a bride to perform "The Goodbye Song" after a wedding luncheon for her new husband. (This song was from the soundtrack of a movie that the couple had just produced about the South Sea island of Pitcairn.) The groom was so surprised that he cried, but he did manage to row his bride, as the music kept repeating, in a flower-bedecked rowboat to an awaiting yacht, and they sailed off into a summer sunset through the Golden Gate Bridge!

Whether you are planning a dinner for four or a midnight supper for fifty, this cookbook and musical cassette will help you create an ambience of romance and elegance. I hope that you'll keep them together on your cookbook shelf.

— Sharon O'Connor

MUSICAL NOTES

The string quartet—first and second violins, viola, and cello—has evolved in Western music for just over two hundred years. During that time composers have chosen it as the medium for some of their most profound and personal musical thoughts. Even with such a great repertoire, the string quartet also has the versatility to perform music that has been composed for other ensembles.

Many of the works presented on the cassette are operatic, orchestral or solo instrumental pieces that have been arranged or transcribed for string quartet. The San Francisco String Quartet has collected these transcriptions and arrangements from many sources during the past ten years, and the quartet members have also made their own arrangements to expand the repertoire. This kind of endeavor has been a common practice of musicians throughout history. Bach himself was an inveterate transcriber both of other composers' music and his own. He adapted unaccompanied pieces for violin or lute into harpsichord concertos, then changed the solo instrumentation to organ so that the music could be fitted into a church cantata. Handel often prepared the "hit" arias of his operas and oratorios for publication as flute and keyboard pieces.

Since the San Francisco String Quartet often performs music for dinners, we have had the chance to introduce or experiment with presenting arrangements not for performance in a concert hall but rather as a musical accompaniment to fine dinners. We've discovered that structuring the musical selections is as important for the success of the evening's entertainment as structuring the menu is to the success of the dinner. The following musical menu selections are based on certain dinner-music fundamentals mixed with the touch of whimsy or humor that brings a fine dinner to life. I am serious about the first menu and hope that you'll enjoy the humor of the second.

MUSICAL MENUS

I

RECEPTION and HORS d'OEUVRES: Bach...Corelli...Handel Tartini...Vivaldi...Mozart

SOUP and FISH COURSE: Handel's *Water Music*...Debussy... Chopin

ENTREE: Haydn...Borodin...Massenet...Beethoven

SALAD: Light and lively encore pieces such as serenades, gavottes, and rondos

CHEESE: Purcell (English cheese)...Debussy, Ravel, Satie (French cheese)

DESSERT: Fritz Kreisler...Lehár...Schubert...J. Strauss

II

COCKTAILS: Scotch on the Rachmaninoff (is one Glazunov?)

HORS d'OEUVRES: Manon l'Escargot...Mousseorgsky Gregorian Chanterelles

SOUP: Porgy and Bouillabess

PASTA: Ravellioli...Noodles Andante...Pizza-cato

ENTREE: Veal a Lobos...La Scalapini...Chicken Khachaturian

VEGETABLES: Mozartichokes...End-Ives...Cornetto on the Cob

SALAD: Pastoral Salad with Polonaisse...Cowell Slaw

CHEESE: Allegro con Brie

DESSERT: Victor Sherbet...Soufflédermaus...Eclair de Lune Rimsky Korsakoffee...CapPuccini

Notes About the Composers

Wolfgang Amadeus Mozart (1756–1791)
First Movement from *Eine Kleine Nachtmusik*

Mozart is regarded as the most universal composer in the history of Western music. He excelled in every musical medium current in his time, especially in chamber music for strings, piano concertos, and opera. *Eine Kleine Nachtmusik (A Little Night Music)* was composed in 1787 while Mozart was in the midst of writing the opera *Don Giovanni,* but no details survive as to why it was written. This serenade is one of Mozart's most perfectly crafted miniatures and is also probably the most widely played piece he composed for strings. It was written for string quartet and bass, but can be successfully performed by a string quartet, since the bass and cello share the bass line.

Johann Sebastian Bach (1685–1750)
Loure from the Third Suite for Unaccompanied Cello
Air and Gavottes from Orchestral Suite in D Major, BWV 1068

Johann Sebastian Bach combined outstanding performing musicianship with supreme creative powers, inventiveness, and intellectual control. As a virtuoso, he achieved lengendary fame in his lifetime, and as a composer he has a unique historical position. He drew together and surmounted the technique, styles, and general musical achievements of his own and earlier generations, and his works have been used by later ages in a great variety of ways. The third movement from the Third Suite for Unaccompanied Cello is one of the most popular movements from Bach's pieces for unaccompanied instruments. It was composed while he was the conductor of the court orchestra of Prince Leopold of Anhalt-Cöthen. During these years of 1717 to 1722, Bach composed a large share of his instrumental music including the *Brandenburg Concertos,* the six suites for unaccompanied cello, and Volume One of *The Well-Tempered*

Clavier. According to the great cellist and humanitarian Pablo Cassals, "The suites for violoncello solo are the quintessence of Bach's creations and Bach himself is the quintessence of all music."

The three transcribed movements from the Orchestral Suite were composed in about 1720. The Air is one of the best known of Bach's compositions. It was popularized by the nineteenth-century violinist August Wilhemj, who transposed it down a ninth and transcribed it for violin and piano as "Air on the G String."

George Frederick Handel (1685–1759)
Suite from *The Water Music*

Handel, a naturalized English composer of German birth, was one of the greatest composers of the Baroque age. His *Water Music* was probably first performed on July 17, 1717. King George I and his courtiers, followed by a large number of boats, sailed on the Thames from Whitehall to Chelsea where they had supper, and then returned by the same route at three in the morning. By the King's request, a second barge containing fifty musicians played works specially composed by Handel. The music was a great success, as an account sent to Prussia two days later reported: "His Majesty approved of it so greatly that he caused it to be repeated three times in all, although each performance lasted an hour—namely twice before and once after supper."

Pietro Mascagni (1863–1945)
Intermezzo Sinfonico from *Cavalleria Rusticana*

Mascagni composed the opera *Cavalleria Rusticana* in 1888. He was almost penniless and completely unknown when he submitted the opera in a competition for one-act operas sponsored by a Milanese publisher. He won the first prize and the world premiere was received with frantic enthusiasm by the audience. *Cavalleria* was soon being performed in opera houses around the world. Unfortunately, in his later works, Mascagni was never able to repeat this first success. The two parts of the action of the opera are linked by a symphonic intermezzo which is heard here as an arrangement for string quartet.

Franz Lehár (1870–1948)
"Merry Widow Waltz"

Lehár, an Austrian composer and conductor, was the leading operetta composer of the twentieth century. Along with Offenbach and Johann Strauss II, he has remained one of the most popular composers of light music. No other operetta conjures up the glamorous pre–World War I Hapsburg Vienna quite like *The Merry Widow (Die Lustige Witwe)*, which he composed in 1905.

Franz Danzi (1763–1826)
"Nach Mozart's Figaro," Op. 6 No. 2

Danzi was a German cellist and composer who wrote mostly for the stage. His works include incidental music, ballet, entr'actes, melodrama, singspiel, and grand opera. He was also a prolific composer of vocal, orchestral, and above all chamber music. This string quartet movement transcribing melodies from the aria of an opera combines his love of opera and chamber music.

Antonio Vivaldi (1678–1741)
First Movement from "Spring" of *The Four Seasons*

Vivaldi was the first great violin virtuoso and the father of the modern concerto. He made the instrument a star performer by his own innovative virtuosity and by modifying the concerto grosso form to allow the violin (and other instruments as well) to function as a solo voice singing out over the orchestra. Vivaldi wrote as many as five hundred concertos for various kinds of instruments. He was also a pioneer of orchestral programme music such as his four concertos portraying the seasons, which he composed in 1725. Printed with *The Four Seasons* was a quartet of sonnets, one for each concerto. The poet is unknown, but they could easily have been written by Vivaldi himself as a guide to the pictorial content of the music. The first two stanzas of the following poem describe the movement recorded on the cassette.

SPRING

Spring has come and joyfully
the birds greet her with merry song,
and brooks blown by the breezes,
sweetly murmuring begin to flow:

Then come, covering the air with a
    black mantle,
lightning and thunder, chosen to herald her,
and when they cease, the tiny birds
take up again their enchanting song.

And after, on the pleasant, flowery meadow,
to the cherished sough of leafy boughs
sleeps the goatherd with his faithful
    dog at his side.

To the joyous sound of the pastoral pipe,
nymphs and shepherds dance in the
    beloved cottage
at the shining appearance of spring.

Luigi Boccherini (1743–1805)
Minuet from String Quintet, Op. 13 No. 5

An Italian composer and cellist, Boccherini was a prolific composer, particularly of chamber music. Along with the string quartet, the string quintet enjoyed great popularity during the second half of the eighteenth century. Boccherini provided lovers of chamber music with a large repertoire of string quintets—almost 150. The "Celebrated Minuet," which he composed in 1771, joins the rare company of beloved short works.

Riccardo Drigo (1846–1930)
"Valse Bluette"

Drigo was an Italian conductor and composer who lived in Russia for more than forty years. He was a conductor and composer for the Imperial Ballet and conducted the first performances of Tchaikovsky's *Sleeping Beauty* and *Nutcracker* ballets. Drigo also composed his own dance scores, which were popular in his day.

Fritz Kreisler (1875–1962)
"Liebesfreud"
"Schön Rosmarin"

There is hardly a violinist in our century who has not acknowledged both admiration and indebtedness to Kreisler. This great virtuoso was also a gifted composer. He composed dozens of pieces in the "olden style" that he ascribed to various eighteenth-century composers such as Pugnani, Francoeur, Martini, etc., and thus became the richest source of "new" short works for the violin in the twentieth century. "Liebesfreud" and "Schön Rosmarin" are two of Kreisler's short pieces that have become household favorites throughout the world.

Johann Strauss II (1825–1899)
Tales of the Vienna Woods

Johann Strauss II, composer, conductor, and violinist, was the most eminent member of the Strauss family. He toured most of Europe with his orchestra and was acclaimed everywhere as Austria's most successful ambassador and the "King of the Waltz." In 1872 he accepted an invitation to go to Boston for an "International Peace Jubilee" confirming the idea of world peace after the end of the Franco-Prussian War. Twenty thousand singers from many countries and ten thousand orchestral musicians assembled for this event. Strauss conducted, with one hundred assistant conductors, a number of waltz sets with an added chorus, and one polka. In 1876

NOCTURNE

he dedicated his *Centennial Waltzes* to the citizens of the United States on the one-hundredth anniversary of the Declaration of Independence.

Strauss composed *Tales of the Vienna Woods* in 1868 during the decade of his "great waltzes," 1860 to 1870. The gaiety and romance of Strauss's music turned Vienna into "the city of dreams" for many.

Alexander Borodin (1833–1887)
Nocturne from String Quartet No. 2

Borodin was a distinguished research chemist and professor in St. Petersburg as well as one of Russia's greatest composers and an amateur cellist. He finished his second String Quartet in 1885 and dedicated it to his wife. His friend and biographer, Serge Dianin, suggests "the *Nocturne* is simply a love scene." This is one of the most famous movements in all chamber music.

:CHEZ:PANISSE:

*T*his "Dinner in the Form of a Classical String Quartet for Sharon O'Connor and the San Francisco String Quartet" was created at Chez Panisse, which is famous for the originality of its menus. Chez Panisse has an international reputation as one of America's truly great restaurants.

• • • • •

Menu

SERVES FOUR

I. ALLEGRO CON FUOCO
Charcoal-grilled Oysters

II. ANDANTE AMOROSO
Artichoke Hearts, Prosciutto, and Fettuccine

III. SCHERZO: ALLEGRO VIVO
Squab Salad with Garden Lettuces

IV. PRESTO
Honey Ice Cream with Lavender

SUGGESTED WINES: Serve a Bandol rosé with the oysters; and a young Beaujolais, served cool, with the artichoke hearts, prosciutto, and fettuccine.

CHARCOAL-GRILLED OYSTERS

SERVES FOUR

2½ dozen oysters

FUMET

1 small carrot
1 small leek
1 small celery rib
½ small onion
2 shallots

Bouquet garni (2 fresh fennel leaves, 3 or 4 parsley sprigs, ½ bay leaf,
    5 or 6 black peppercorns)
4 or 5 chervil stems

SAUCE

¼ pound unsalted butter
½ cup *fumet*
1 tablespoon heavy cream
Fresh lemon juice and ground white pepper to taste

Rock salt
Handful of chervil sprigs
2 to 3 ounces yellow whitefish caviar

Shuck a dozen of the oysters and save their liquor to make the *fumet*.
Cut the carrot, leek, celery, and onion into quarters. Roughly dice the
shallots. Tie up the *bouquet* ingredients in a cheesecloth. Put the dozen
shucked oysters and their liquor, the wine, the vegetables, and the *bouquet garni* in a stainless steel or enameled pot and cover with cold
water. Bring to a boil, reduce the heat immediately, and skim and
simmer for half an hour. Strain the *fumet,* add the chervil stems,
and reduce by one-third.

To make the sauce, the butter should be a little cooler than room temperature. Cut the butter into tablespoon-sized pieces. Take the chervil stems out of the *fumet* and measure ½ cup of the *fumet* into a heavy saucepan. Bring to a boil, reduce the heat, and whisk in the butter bit by bit as you would for a *beurre blanc*. Add the cream and the lemon juice and pepper to taste. The sauce should have a light syrupy texture.

Heat a grill with mesquite charcoal so that the flame is licking about an inch over the grill. Meanwhile, heat a platter or a shallow casserole that is large enough to hold the remaining oysters and spread with ½ inch of rock salt. Heat the salt in a very hot oven for 15 minutes. When the fire is ready, put the remaining 1½ dozen oysters directly on the grill, curved side down. When the shells just open slightly or begin bubbling (in 2 to 4 minutes), remove the oysters from the fire. Finish opening them with an oyster knife and discard the flat top shell. Arrange the oysters on the hot rock salt and put a teaspoon or so of the sauce over each one. Garnish each oyster with a sprig of chervil and half a teaspoon or so of caviar.

ARTICHOKE HEARTS, PROSCIUTTO, AND FETTUCCINE

SERVES FOUR

1½ pounds baby artichokes
Juice of 1 lemon
1 cup fresh bread crumbs
10 to 12 tablespoons virgin olive oil
1 onion, diced
3 garlic cloves, chopped
Salt and ground black pepper
A handful fresh parsley leaves, chopped
A handful fresh basil leaves, chopped
¼ pound thinly sliced prosciutto, cut into thin strips
1 pound fettuccine
¼ to ½ cup freshly grated Parmesan cheese

continued

Prepare the artichokes by first cutting off the top third of the leaves. Pull off the tough outer leaves, exposing the tender center. Pare around the bottom with a small knife, removing the dark-green base of the leaves. Cut the bottoms into quarters and put them into water to cover that has been acidulated with the lemon juice. These small artichokes are immature enough that the chokes have not yet developed, so all but the exterior is edible. Toast the bread crumbs in a 300° oven until dry and lightly browned, then toss them with 3 or 4 tablespoons of the olive oil.

In a sauté pan, sauté the onion and garlic in 3 or 4 tablespoons of the olive oil. Add the artichokes, season with salt and pepper to taste, cover, and braise slowly until tender (approximately 15 to 20 minutes). Add the parsley, basil, prosciutto, and another 4 tablespoons of the olive oil. Cook the fettuccine in a large quantity of boiling salted water until *al dente*. Drain. Toss with the artichoke mixture. Season with additional black pepper. Serve garnished with the toasted bread crumbs and Parmesan cheese.

SQUAB SALAD WITH GARDEN LETTUCES

SERVES FOUR

½ cup virgin olive oil
2 squabs, about 1 pound each, livers reserved
1 tablespoon unsalted butter
6 tablespoons Armagnac
¼ cup squab or chicken stock
2 teaspoons port
4 shallots, minced
Reserved pan juices from the squab
Salt and pepper to taste
1 tablespoon to ¼ cup sherry vinegar
Minced black truffle (optional)
1 tablespoon walnut oil (optional)
4 big handfuls of little lettuces and salad herbs (rocket, garden cress, chicory, watercress, dandelion greens, and red leaf or oak leaf lettuces)

To cook the squabs, heat 3 tablespoons of the olive oil in a skillet over medium-high heat and brown them, turning frequently. Add the butter halfway through the browning. When the squabs are browned (about 7 minutes), flame the pan with 3 tablespoons of the Armagnac. When the flame dies, put the squab in a roasting pan, breast up. Pour off the oil from the sauté pan and deglaze with the stock and port. Roast the squab in a preheated 475° oven, basting them 3 or 4 times with the deglazing juices, for 12 to 15 minutes. They are done when the breast meat is still quite pink. Cool them at room temperature and reserve all the juices.

Heat 1 tablespoon of the olive oil in a sauté pan over medium-high heat and sauté the reserved livers with three-fourths of the shallots. Turn the livers once or twice and sauté for 1 or 2 minutes only. Flame the pan with the remaining 3 tablespoons of Armagnac and add the reserved juices from the roast squab. Remove the livers to cool at room temperature and strain the pan juices.

In a mixing bowl, mix the remaining shallots with the remaining 4 tablespoons of olive oil, the reserved pan juices, and salt and pepper and vinegar to taste. The amount of vinegar will depend on the strength of the squab juices. Let this vinaigrette stand 15 to 20 minutes, then strain. Add the truffles and the walnut oil, if desired, and correct the seasoning.

To assemble the salad, remove the breasts from the squab and slice each breast on a diagonal into ⅜-inch slices. Slice the livers into ⅜-inch slices. Reserve the juices from slicing and stir them into the vinaigrette. Toss the lettuce leaves with enough vinaigrette to coat them lightly, and put them on salad plates. Arrange the breasts on the lettuce and garnish the salad with the livers.

Honey Ice Cream with Lavender

SERVES FOUR

4 cups heavy cream
½ cup strong-flavored honey (thyme, heather, or Tupelo is good)
5 egg yolks
A few lavender blossoms (optional)

Mix together 3 cups of the cream, the honey, and egg yolks, and cook in a double boiler over very hot water, stirring constantly with a wooden spoon until the mixture coats the spoon, about 10 minutes. Add the lavender blossoms the last minute or two of the cooking time. Strain the mixture and stir in the remaining cup of cream. Cover and chill completely, then freeze in an ice cream freezer.

CULINARY COMPANY

*J*udith Ets-Hokin founded the Judith Ets- Hokin Culinary Company in 1972. She has studied with Paul Meyer and Paul Quiaud in the United States and has certificates from Cordon Bleu in London and from cooking schools in Dieppe, France, and Florence, Italy. She is the author of *The San Francisco Dinner Party Cookbook* and director of The Judith Ets-Hokin Cooking School.

Judith introduces her menu as follows:

"This is an impressive and elegant meal that can be prepared almost entirely in advance. The cake may be made as much as a day before serving. You can finish preparing the scallops several hours ahead of time, placing them in individual serving dishes on a baking sheet, ready to be warmed. Before the guests arrive, finish roasting the lamb and let it rest in a warm place, covered loosely with foil until ready to carve and serve. (If the lamb has cooled, reheat it in the oven 15 to 20 minutes before carving.) About one hour before you plan to serve the eggplant and lamb, pour the custard over the eggplant and put it into the oven.

"As soon as the eggplant is baked, invite your guests to the table and serve the scallops. The eggplant needs about 20 minutes' rest in a warm place before cutting. It will wait patiently while you are enjoying the first course. Be sure to serve the main course on warmed plates. The salad may be tossed and served at the table. And please serve the hazelnut cake at the table. Watching the cake being cut and served is enjoyed by all.

"Be prepared for raves!"

• • • • •

Menu

SEA SCALLOPS *in* SHALLOT CREAM

ROAST BUTTERFLIED LAMB

EGGPLANT PIE

WATERCRESS *and* ENDIVE SALAD

HAZELNUT MERINGUE CAKE *with*
APRICOT-CREAM FILLING

SUGGESTED WINES: A white Bordeaux with the scallops; and
a red Bordeaux, a Graves, or a California Gamay with the lamb.

SEA SCALLOPS IN SHALLOT CREAM

SERVES EIGHT

1½ cups dry white wine
Bouquet garni (2 parsley sprigs, ½ bay leaf, and 1 thyme sprig, tied
   with string)
1 pound sea scallops, rinsed
6 tablespoons unsalted butter
½ pound mushrooms, sliced
6 shallots, minced
4 tablespoons minced fresh parsley
1 tablespoon fresh lemon juice
1 tablespoon flour
3 to 4 tablespoons *crème fraîche*
Salt and pepper to taste
½ pound cooked tiny shrimp

In a medium saucepan, bring the wine and *bouquet garni* to a boil, add
the scallops, and simmer for 1 minute. Drain the scallops, reserving the
liquid, and cut them into 1-inch pieces. Melt 2 tablespoons of the butter
in a saucepan; add the mushrooms, shallots, 2 tablespoons of the
parsley, and lemon juice. Cover and simmer for 10 minutes. Drain the
mushrooms and add the liquid to the wine broth. Melt the remaining
butter in a saucepan, add the flour, and cook over medium heat for 2
minutes. Add the combined liquids and cook the sauce over low heat
until it is thickened and smooth, approximately 30 minutes. Add the
crème fraîche. Taste the sauce for seasoning and add salt and pepper to
taste.

Combine the sauce with the scallops, mushrooms, and cooked shrimp.
Spoon into 8 individual ovenproof servers (porcelain or natural scallop
shells), piling the scallops high in the center. Just before serving, heat in
a preheated 450° oven for 5 minutes. Garnish each serving with a little
of the remaining parsley.

ROAST BUTTERFLIED LAMB

SERVES EIGHT TO TEN

3 tablespoons mixed dry white, green, and black peppercorns, crushed
1 fresh rosemary sprig
4 fresh mint sprigs
5 garlic cloves, crushed
½ cup raspberry vinegar
4 tablespoons soy sauce
⅔ cup dry white wine
One 5-pound leg of lamb, boned and left flat
4 tablespoons Dijon mustard
Rosemary and mint sprigs for garnish

Combine half the peppercorns with all of the rosemary, mint, garlic, vinegar, soy sauce, and wine. Marinate the lamb 24 hours in the refrigerator. Remove the lamb from the marinade, pat dry, and reserve the marinade. Combine the remaining peppercorns and the mustard to make a paste. Spread the paste over the meat, skin side up. Leave the meat untied, place in a shallow roasting dish, and spoon the reserved marinade around the lamb.

Roast the lamb at 450° for 50 minutes for rare, 1 hour for medium rare, basting approximately 2 times during the roasting. Let the roast stand 20 minutes before carving. Overlap the slices of lamb on the plate, spoon the pan juices over all, and garnish with the rosemary and mint.

EGGPLANT PIE

SERVES EIGHT TO TWELVE

1 eggplant, about 1 pound
1 teaspoon salt
Vegetable oil
Salt and ground black pepper to taste
1 tablespoon minced fresh parsley
Pinch thyme
3 medium tomatoes, sliced
½ onion, chopped
1 green pepper, chopped
8 ounces Gruyère cheese, sliced
3 eggs
1½ cups *crème fraîche*

Peel and slice the eggplant, sprinkle with salt, and let stand 1 hour. Pat dry, place on a baking sheet, brush on a little oil, and broil 3 minutes on each side. Place the eggplant slices on the bottom of a 9-by-12-inch ovenproof dish. Sprinkle with salt, pepper, parsley, and thyme. Cover with the tomatoes. Sprinkle with salt, pepper, onion, and green pepper. Place the cheese slices over all.

Whisk the eggs and combine with the *crème fraîche.* Approximately 45 minutes before serving, pour the custard over the eggplant and bake uncovered in a 350° oven for about 45 minutes or until set. Cut in squares to serve.

WATERCRESS AND ENDIVE SALAD

2 bunches watercress
2 heads Belgian endive

DRESSING
¾ cup walnut oil
½ teaspoon each salt, pepper, and sugar
3 tablespoons red wine vinegar
1 tablespoon Dijon mustard

Remove the stems from the watercress and slice the endive thinly,
discarding the root ends. Crisp the greens in the refrigerator. Combine
the dressing ingredients. Just before serving, toss the greens with the
dressing. Serve immediately.

Hazelnut Meringue Cake
with Apricot-Cream Filling

SERVES EIGHT TO TWELVE

CAKE

1½ cups whole hazelnuts
4 egg whites
1 cup sugar
1 tablespoon flour
1 tablespoon vanilla extract

FILLING

½ cup dried apricots, soaked overnight in water to barely cover
4 tablespoons sugar
Juice of half a lemon
1 cup *crème fraîche*

Powdered sugar

To make the cake, toast the hazelnuts 3 to 5 minutes on a baking sheet in a 350° oven. Whisk the egg whites until they hold soft peaks. Gradually add the sugar, continuing to whisk until firmer peaks form. Grind the hazelnuts in a blender with the flour and fold into the meringue. Fold in the vanilla. Pour the batter into two 8-inch greased floured round cake pans and bake approximately 1 hour in a preheated 325° oven until delicately browned and crisp. Cool in the pans for 3 to 5 minutes, remove from the pans, and finish cooling the cakes on racks.

To make the filling, place the apricots, sugar, and lemon juice in a saucepan and simmer gently 30 to 60 minutes until soft enough to sieve. Force through a sieve with the back of a large spoon. Whip the *crème fraîche* and carefully fold in the sieved apricots.

Spread the cream generously on one layer of the cake. Add the top layer and sprinkle with powdered sugar. Any remaining cream can be served on the side. Chill the cake several hours before serving.

COW HOLLOW CATERING CO.

*I*n 1972, Judy and Norman Sawicki began Cow Hollow Catering, which specializes in California and ethnic cuisine. Emphasis is placed on obtaining the highest quality and freshest ingredients available for parties which range in size from ten to three thousand guests. The Sawickis have owned several restaurants in San Francisco and currently own a popular Napa Valley restaurant.

• • • • •

MENU

PESTO-STUFFED MUSHROOMS

GOLDEN CAVIAR on MINI TOASTS

CARROT and TOMATO SOUP

COULIBIACS of SEA BASS with
TARRAGON BEURRE BLANC

SAUTEED BABY VEGETABLES

WATERCRESS and ENDIVE SALAD with
AVOCADO and TOMATO

CHOCOLATE MOUSSE PIE

SUGGESTED WINES: A brut Champagne with the caviar; and
a California Chardonnay or Sauvignon Blanc with the *coulibiacs*.

Pesto-stuffed Mushrooms

SERVES TEN

10 large mushrooms, stems removed
4 tablespoons butter
1 tablespoon fresh lemon juice

FILLING

4 ounces cream cheese at room temperature
¼ cup *pesto* (frozen or homemade)
½ teaspoon minced fresh thyme, or ¼ teaspoon dried thyme
½ teaspoon minced fresh oregano, or ¼ teaspoon dried oregano
Salt to taste

Pine nuts

In a sauté pan, lightly sauté the mushroom caps in butter and lemon juice for 2 minutes on each side. Transfer them from the pan to a platter and let cool while making the filling. Cream together the cheese, *pesto,* herbs, and salt until fluffy. Put into a pastry bag with a star tip (or other decorative tip) and pipe into the cooled mushroom caps. Decorate the center of each mushroom with a whole pine nut. These can be made a day in advance of the party.

Golden Caviar on Mini Toasts

SERVES TEN

1 package Cressa Mini Toasts
1 cup sour cream
4 ounces golden caviar
3 green onions, green tops only, minced

Spread the mini toasts with sour cream (not too thickly). Top each with about ¼ to ½ teaspoon of golden caviar and sprinkle with minced green onions.

Carrot and Tomato Soup

SERVES TEN

2 pounds carrots, coarsely chopped
4 tablespoons butter
8 cups chicken stock
6 tablespoons tomato purée
½ cup finely grated potatoes
2 egg yolks
2 tablespoons milk
1 leek, cut into fine julienne and blanched

In a large saucepan, sauté the carrots in the butter for about 3 minutes. Add 2 cups of the stock and simmer for about 15 minutes, or until the carrots are tender. Purée in a blender or food processor until smooth. Stir in the tomato purée, remaining stock, and potatoes. Simmer for 15 minutes. Beat together the egg yolks and milk. Add ½ cup of the hot soup to the mixture, then pour it into the soup. *Do not let the soup boil after the egg mixture is added.* Ladle into heated soup bowls or a soup tureen and garnish with the julienned leek.

COULIBIACS OF SEA BASS WITH TARRAGON BEURRE BLANC

SERVES TEN

4 teaspoons quick-cooking tapioca
½ cup dry white wine
4 hard-cooked eggs
1⅓ cups cooked rice
3 tablespoons minced fresh dill weed
Salt and pepper to taste
2 tablespoons butter
2 tablespoons oil
2½ pounds fillet of sea bass, cut into 10 pieces, each about 3½ by
   2 inches
1 box *filo* dough
1 cup melted butter
Tarragon Beurre Blanc, following

Soak the tapioca in the wine for 5 minutes, then simmer over low heat for 5 minutes. Mince 2 of the hard-cooked eggs and the yolks from the 2 remaining hard-cooked eggs (reserve the 2 whites for another use). Combine the rice, eggs, dill, salt, and pepper with the tapioca mixture. Melt the butter with the oil in a heavy skillet and sauté the sea bass pieces over very high heat for 1 minute per side. Remove and set aside.

   Working quickly so the dough does not dry out, brush one sheet of *filo* with melted butter, fold it in half, and brush again with butter. Place about 2½ to 3 tablespoons of the rice mixture 1 inch in from one of the short edges, then top with one piece of sea bass. Fold in the long edges, then roll to form an envelope. Place the finished *coulibiac* on a baking sheet and brush the top with melted butter. Do likewise for the remaining pieces of fish. Bake the *coulibiacs* for 20 minutes in a preheated 375° oven. Serve with tarragon *beurre blanc*.

Tarragon Beurre Blanc

6 shallots, minced
2 tablespoons minced fresh tarragon
¾ cup dry white wine
¼ cup white wine vinegar
1 pound butter, cut into tablespoon-sized portions

In a heavy saucepan, cook the shallots and tarragon with the wine and vinegar until the liquid is reduced to ⅓ cup. Take off the heat and whisk in the butter 1 tablespoon at a time until thoroughly incorporated. Keep the sauce warm, but do not let it boil.

Sautéed Baby Vegetables

SERVES TEN

4 tablespoons butter
2½ to 3 pounds baby vegetables
Salt and pepper to taste

Melt the butter in a sauté pan and sauté the vegetables over medium-high heat. (Make sure that the vegetables that are thicker or take longer to cook are added to the pan first.) Cook until just tender, usually only a few minutes. Season and serve immediately.

CHOCOLATE MOUSSE PIE

SERVES TEN

CRUST

1 package Nabisco chocolate wafers
½ cup melted butter

FILLING

1 pound semisweet chocolate
6 eggs
2 cups heavy cream
4 tablespoons powdered sugar

TOPPING

1 cup heavy cream
4 tablespoons powdered sugar
Candied violets for garnish

To make the crust, put the cookies in a blender or food processor and process until they are in fine crumbs. Add the melted butter and process until just mixed. Press the crumb mixture on the bottom and sides of a 10-inch springform pan. Refrigerate while making the filling.

To make the filling, melt the chocolate in a double boiler over barely simmering water. Cool to lukewarm and transfer to a blender or food processor. Separate the eggs. Add 2 whole eggs and 4 yolks to the chocolate and blend until smooth. Whip the 4 egg whites until stiff but not dry. Whip the cream with the powdered sugar until soft peaks form. Add one-quarter of the whipped egg whites and the whipped cream to the chocolate and blend until the mixture is thoroughly blended.

Pour the chocolate mixture into a large bowl and carefully fold in the whipped cream and then the egg whites. Pour into the chilled pie shell and refrigerate for at least 6 hours or overnight.

When ready to serve, make the topping. Whip the cream and the sugar. Loosen and remove the sides of the pan and spread half of the whipped cream over the top of the pie. Put the remaining half into a pastry bag with a decorative tip and pipe around the edge. Garnish with candied violets.

E D I B L E · A R T

*E*dible Art was created in 1980 by Sharon Polster and Robin McMillan with the view that food is an artistic medium. Their combination of quality ingredients and stylized presentation has served clients worldwide, including Paloma Picasso, the Fine Arts Museums of San Francisco, and the cast of *Dynasty*. Sharon Polster did the beautiful food styling for our cover and she also offered me this personal expression as an introduction to her spring menu:

"What is it 'to entertain'? Edible Art's definition is to amuse; to show panache with the style of any event. It is transcending the usual by taking an environment, the decor, good food and wine, and beautiful music to create a total ambience. It is taking an occasion, a theme or a season and artfully balancing the components of a concept. In short, it is making a fantasy come to life.

"Spring is a wonderful season for fantasies. A scene that comes to mind is a twilight supper in the midst of a flowering meadow. The food echoes spring's new crop abundance, the wine is crisp, and Vivaldi's vision of 'Spring' from his *Four Seasons* is being played in the background."

• • • • •

MENU

LOBSTER-MANGO SAUTE

SPRING LAMB FILETS with ITALIAN MUSHROOMS,
ASPARAGUS, and SAUCE CHAUSSEUR

BABY LETTUCE with SCENTED GERANIUM SORBET

PEAR-HAZELNUT SOUFFLE
with CREME ANGLAISE

SUGGESTED WINES: An Alsatian Tokay or a dry Gewürztraminer with the scallops; and a French Burgundy or a California Pinot Noir with the lamb.

LOBSTER-MANGO SAUTÉ

SERVES FOURTEEN

Fourteen 8-ounce lobster tails
2 pounds snow peas
1 bunch basil
1 cup butter
4 shallots, minced
4 garlic cloves, minced
4 tablespoons gold tequila
6 mangoes, peeled, sliced, and cut into 1-inch dice
Salt, pepper, and cayenne to taste

Cut the upper shell down the center of each lobster back with scissors, leaving the tail fan intact. Do not remove the under shell. Lift the uncooked tail through the slit and spread the shell. Cut the lobster meat into 1-inch cubes.

Take the stems and tails off the snow peas and blanch the peas for 30 seconds. Run them under cold water to stop the cooking and drain. Julienne the basil leaves.

In a large sauté pan, melt half of the butter. Add half of the shallots and garlic and sauté over medium heat until translucent. Then add 2 tablespoons of the tequila and deglaze the pan over high heat. Add half of the lobster and mangoes and sauté over high heat for 2 minutes. Remove from the pan with a slotted spoon and place in a large container. Melt the remaining butter and sauté the remaining shallots and garlic until translucent. Deglaze the pan with the remaining tequila and sauté the remaining lobster and mangoes over high heat for 2 minutes. Add the mixture to the previous mixture and season with cayenne, salt, and pepper to taste. Put the mixture back into the lobster tails and garnish with the basil.

Place snow peas in circular pattern around the edge of each salad plate. Place a filled lobster tail in the middle of the snow peas.

Spring Lamb Filets with Italian Mushrooms, Asparagus, and Sauce Chausseur

SERVES FOURTEEN

5 racks of lamb
2 tablespoons minced fresh parsley and rosemary
5 garlic cloves, minced
1 teaspoon pepper
6 tablespoons butter
½ pound fresh *pleurette* mushrooms or fresh button mushrooms
1 fresh *porto bello* mushroom or any large fresh mushroom
½ cup butter
2 shallots, chopped
Fresh-ground pepper
56 asparagus spears
Sauce Chausseur, following

Trim the lamb of any fat. Cut the meat off the racks in one piece. Mix together the herbs, garlic, and pepper. Sprinkle the mixture over the lamb and pat. Melt the butter in a sauté pan and sauté the filets over medium-high heat until browned (about 2 minutes per side). Transfer to a baking sheet and bake in a 375° oven for 5 minutes.

Stem the *pleurettes*; cut into ¼-inch-thick slices. Stem the *porto bello* mushroom and cut into ¼-inch-thick slices, leaving them in long strips. In a sauté pan, heat ¼ cup of the butter and sauté half of the shallots until translucent. Add the *porto bello* mushroom strips and sauté for about 2 minutes. In another sauté pan heat the remaining butter and sauté the remaining shallots until translucent. Add the *pleurette* mushrooms and sauté for about 2 minutes. Season with fresh-ground pepper.

Cut the stalks off the asparagus spears, leaving 3 to 4 inches of tip. Blanch the asparagus until crisp-tender, about 2 minutes, depending on the size of the asparagus.

Slice each lamb filet in 9 slices (3 per person). Place the lamb in a circular "flower" pattern around the plate. Place 1 asparagus tip between each slice of lamb. Place 1 strip of *porto bello* mushroom in the middle of the lamb "flower." Top each lamb slice with a slice of *pleurette* mushroom. Ladle *chausseur* sauce over each lamb serving.

SAUCE CHAUSSEUR

MAKES ABOUT 2½ CUPS

2 tablespoons butter
3 tablespoons olive oil
12 medium-sized mushrooms, minced
2 teaspoons shallots, minced
2 cups dry white wine
1 cup brandy
½ cup tomato sauce
2 cups *demi-glace**
1 tablespoon chopped fresh parsley

Heat the butter and olive oil in a saucepan. Sauté the mushrooms
quickly until slightly browned. Add the shallots and immediately
remove half of the butter and oil. Pour in the white wine and brandy.
Reduce the liquid by half. Finish the sauce by adding the tomato sauce
and *demi-glace*. Boil for 5 minutes and stir in the chopped parsley.

* *Demi-glace* is a reduction of beef stock, onions, carrots, wine, and seasonings.

BABY LETTUCE SALAD

SERVES FOURTEEN

DRESSING

Juice and grated zest of 1 lemon
½ cup oil
1 teaspoon sugar
1 teaspoon Dijon mustard
Salt and pepper to taste

Leaves from 5 heads baby lettuce
14 *radicchio* leaves, trimmed into "cups"

Scented Geranium Sorbet, following
Rose-scented geranium petals or rose petals

Whisk all the dressing ingredients together. Tear the baby lettuce leaves into pieces and toss with the dressing. Place the tossed leaves on each salad plate. Put a *radicchio* leaf in the center of the lettuces. Place 1 scoop of *sorbet* in the radicchio "cup." Garnish with flower petals.

SCENTED GERANIUM SORBET

MAKES ABOUT 5 CUPS

4 cups Chardonnay wine
½ cup rosewater
½ cup simple syrup
Petals from 10 rose-scented geraniums or 10 roses

Chill an ice-cream maker for 5 minutes. Mix the wine, rosewater, and simple syrup together; pour into the ice-cream machine. Churn the *sorbet* for 20 minutes. Add the geranium or rose petals. Continue to freeze for another 10 to 15 minutes or until the *sorbet* is fluffy. Pack into a container, cover, and freeze.

* To make simple syrup, boil 1 part water to 2 parts sugar for 5 minutes.

Pear-Hazelnut Soufflé with Crème Anglaise

SERVES FOURTEEN

5 firm but ripe pears, peeled and cored
½ cup butter
½ cup brown sugar
¾ cup hazelnuts
1 cup milk
3 egg yolks
3 tablespoons sugar
3 tablespoons flour
⅛ teaspoon salt
3 tablespoons butter
½ teaspoon vanilla extract
4 egg whites
Crème Anglaise, following

Cut the pears into ½-inch dice. In a sauté pan over medium-high heat, melt the butter and sauté the pears for about 2 minutes. Sprinkle the pears with brown sugar, tossing well. Continue to sauté the pears for 5 minutes or until they are glazed and browned.

Fit fourteen 12-ounce soufflé cups with 2-inch foil collars. Butter the cups and the collars and sprinkle lightly with sugar. Place equal amounts of pear cubes in the bottom of each cup.

Grind the hazelnuts with a nut grinder. Heat the milk to just below the boiling point and pour over the nuts. Beat the egg yolks until light. Gradually beat into the egg yolks the sugar, flour, and salt. Stir a small quantity of the hot mixture into the eggs and then return this combination to the rest of the hot mixture. Stir and cook these ingredients over low heat to permit the yolks to thicken slightly. Stir in the butter. Cool the mixture. Beat in the vanilla. Beat the egg whites until stiff but not dry. Fold the egg whites into the cooled custard. Spoon the mixture over the pear cubes in the soufflé cups. Bake in a preheated 350° oven for 30 minutes. Remove the collars and serve with *crème anglaise*.

Crème Anglaise

2⅔ cups milk
1 teaspoon vanilla extract
10 egg yolks
1⅓ cups sugar

In a large, heavy saucepan, bring the milk to the scalding point. Turn off the heat and add the vanilla. In a bowl, beat the egg yolks with the sugar until they are pale, thick, and frothy. Slowly add the hot milk and vanilla, whisking constantly. Pour the mixture back into the saucepan and cook over low heat, stirring constantly. As the sauce heats it will become thicker and coat the spoon. When it reaches the boiling point, remove it from the heat and pour it into a bowl placed over ice water. Stir until it reaches room temperature. Cover and refrigerate.

Timothy Maxson, creator of Taste, views food at its best as an evolving art form. He combines superb cuisine and visually beautiful presentations in his work. The menu and recipes for this project were created at Taste by chef Ted Smith, who also presented me with the following wonderful statement:

"Being a musician as well as a cook (and a big eater), music and food have never been too distantly separated in my mind. I get the same sort of thrill from a beautifully presented meal as from a beautiful performance of Mozart. This menu, to me, reflects the feelings and flavors of Central Europe. With it I pay homage to the sounds of the Mediterranean countries and the area northward from the Balkans all the way to the Alps.

"In particular, I hear something deep and brooding, with a Mediterranean flavor, for the first course. The sorbet was undeniably inspired by Dvorak's 'Humoresque.' The piquancy and vibrant colors of the entrée would be well served by Enesco's 'Roumanian Rhapsody No. 1' or Liszt's 'Hungarian Rhapsody.'

"The salad asks for a lighthearted tarantella or some such Italian country fare, and the dessert bubbles away to the strains of Lehár or J. Strauss.

"Ultimately, art is an expression of life, and what is more important to life than good food for the body and good music for the soul?"

• • • • •

Menu

PRELUDE
Grilled Marinated Calamari
with Tapenade

INTERMEZZO
Beet-Dill Sorbet

SECONDO
Stuffed Pork Tenderloin
on a Bed of Green and Yellow Pipérade

Braised Red Cabbage
with Goat Cheese

CODA
Spinach and Watercress Salad
with Blood Orange Dressing

FINALE
Fresh Kadota Figs and Raspberries
with Pink Champagne Sabayon

SUGGESTED WINES: A California Blanc de Noir with the
calamari; and a Hungarian red or a California Cabernet Sauvignon with
the pork.

GRILLED MARINATED CALAMARI WITH TAPENADE

SERVES TWENTY-FOUR

2 cups mild olive oil
6 garlic cloves, crushed
10 mint sprigs, crushed
10 whole peppercorns
¼ cup fresh lemon juice
24 squid
Tapenade, following
24 mint sprigs

In a medium sacuepan, heat the oil over low heat to 150° F. Add the garlic, mint, and pepper. Remove from the heat. Cool completely. When cool, add the lemon juice.

Wash the squid. Hold the base of the tentacles in one hand and the tail in the other and pull apart. Pull out the cuttle bone and the ink sac. Cut off the tentacles above the eyes. Discard the eyes, innards, and round cartilage at the base of the tentacles. Remove the outer pigmented membrane. Rinse and thread each squid on 2 parallel skewers. Place the skewers in a shallow nonreactive pan large enough to hold them comfortably. Pour the marinade over. Marinate in the refrigerator overnight. Drain and grill very briefly (30 seconds on each side) over mesquite, or broil for the same amount of time. Serve with a small dollop of the *tapenade* and a sprig of mint. Serve hot or at room temperature.

TAPENADE

MAKES 1 QUART

2 pounds pitted oil-cured black olives
2 tablespoons roasted garlic purée,* or 1 tablespoon fresh garlic purée
Two 2-ounce tins anchovies, drained

½ cup capers, drained
6 tablespoons olive oil
3 tablespoons chopped fresh mint

Blend all the ingredients in a blender or food processor to a smooth paste. Store covered in a glass or ceramic container in the refrigerator for at least 24 hours before serving. Keeps indefinitely.

* To make roasted garlic purée, cut off the tops of the cloves of 1 head of garlic and rub them with olive oil. Wrap the head in aluminum foil and bake it in a 350° oven for 45 minutes to 1 hour. Squeeze out the soft garlic and run it through a sieve. 1 head = 1 tablespoon paste.

BEET-DILL SORBET

SERVES TWENTY-FOUR

1⅓ cups sugar
1 cup water
⅓ cup fresh lemon juice
2 to 2½ pounds beets, cooked, drained, peeled, and puréed (4 cups of purée)
1 cup frozen orange juice concentrate
¼ cup full-bodied dry red wine
2 teaspoons kosher salt
2 tablespoons chopped fresh dill weed
Mint sprigs

Combine the sugar, water, and lemon juice in a heavy saucepan over medium to high heat. Bring just to a boil and remove from the heat. Cool completely and chill.

Combine all the remaining ingredients and chill. Stir in the syrup. Freeze in an ice cream freezer or still-freeze by placing the mixture in a shallow (2-inch) baking pan for 24 hours. Blend in a blender or food processor and refreeze. Blend again several hours before serving. Serve each portion with a fresh mint sprig.

STUFFED PORK TENDERLOIN

SERVES TWENTY-FOUR

One 10-pound boneless pork tenderloin
2 tablespoons freshly ground black pepper
2 tablespoons sweet paprika
1 tablespoon minced fresh thyme, or 1 teaspoon dried thyme
4 pounds dry German (garlic) sausage, cut into 24 pieces
1 pound thinly sliced lean bacon or caul fat

Trim the tenderloin and cut it into 24 portions across the grain. Make a lengthwise horizontal slit through the middle of each portion. Mix the spices in a small bowl and rub each portion of pork inside and out. Stuff each portion with a piece of sausage and wrap with the bacon or caul fat. Roast on a rack in a preheated 425° to 450° oven for 15 to 20 minutes. Run under a broiler to lightly brown if necessary. The pork may also be grilled over mesquite if the bacon or caul fat is secured with a skewer. Serve on a bed of Green and Yellow Bell Pipérade, following.

Green and Yellow Bell Pipérade

Serves Twenty-Four

1¼ pounds lean bacon
1 cup butter
⅔ cups olive oil
2 or 3 large onions (3 pounds), chopped
5 pounds yellow (golden) bell peppers, sliced
3 pounds green bell peppers, sliced
6 garlic cloves, minced
2 teaspoons salt
1 teaspoon sugar
Generous pinch of ground caraway
Cayenne to taste

Cook the bacon until it begins to brown. Remove the bacon with a slotted spatula. In the same pan, melt the butter with the olive oil. Add the onions and sauté until they are golden and most of the liquid has evaporated. Lower the heat and add the peppers and garlic. Sauté lightly until the peppers just begin to soften. Crumble the bacon and add to the pan. Add the salt, sugar, caraway, and cayenne. Reheat just before serving.

Braised Red Cabbage with Goat Cheese

SERVES TWENTY-FOUR

½ cup unsalted butter
2 tablespoons olive oil
2 medium heads red cabbage, finely shredded
1 cup chicken stock
1 tablespoon fennel seed, crushed
Pinch of cinnamon
8 ounces mild goat cheese, crumbled

Melt the butter in a large skillet with the olive oil over high heat. When foaming, add the cabbage and toss to coat. Sauté until heated through. Add the chicken stock (it should sizzle when it hits the pan). Add the fennel and cinnamon and continue to toss until the liquid is evaporated and the cabbage is still crisp-tender and brightly colored. Keep warm. Add the goat cheese and toss just before serving.

Spinach and Watercress Salad with Blood Orange Dressing

SERVES TWENTY-FOUR

DRESSING

2 cups olive oil
¾ cup blood orange juice
¼ cup fresh lemon juice
1 tablespoon roasted garlic purée (see page 63), or 1 minced garlic
  clove
1 tablespoon chopped fresh basil
½ teaspoon salt
Cayenne to taste

6 bunches spinach, stemmed
6 bunches watercress, stemmed
4 blood oranges, each cut into 6 slices, for garnish

To make the dressing, whisk together the oil and juices by alternating
¼-cup measures. Add the garlic purée and basil and then add the salt
and cayenne.

Toss the spinach and watercress leaves with the dressing to coat them
lightly and put them on the salad plates. Garnish each salad with a slice
of blood orange.

Fresh Kadota Figs and Raspberries with Pink Champagne Sabayon

SERVES TWENTY-FOUR

SABAYON

35 egg yolks
4 cups sifted powdered sugar
4 cups flat pink champagne (Schramsberg Blanc de Noir is nice)
2 tablespoons kirsch

48 Kadota figs

Combine the yolks and sugar in the top of a double boiler over low to medium heat. Whisk constantly until the mixture begins to thicken. Add the champagne and kirsch gradually. Continue to whisk until thickened to desired sauce consistency. Halve the figs and arrange 2 on each serving plate in a pool of sauce. Make a small indentation with your little finger in the middle of each fig and stuff it with a raspberry. Mound a few more berries in the center of the plate. Serve with the same champagne used in the sauce.

PARTIES, PARTIES, PARTIES.

*P*arties, Parties, Parties was founded in 1978 by Donna Balsamo because she wanted to create celebrations featuring the finest cuisine combined with theatrical excitement. A favorite theme party of hers is "An Evening with the Silver Kings," set in a beautiful San Francisco Pacific Heights mansion built by James Flood at the turn of the century. This evening of elegance features a menu that might have been served by Flood, a Comstock baron, with California wines flowing and a lavish midnight buffet accompanied by the music of the San Francisco String Quartet. The menu, selected from San Francisco's diverse culinary history, was prepared by Parties, Parties, Parties chefs Betsy Ayers and Marty Rosenblum.

• • • • •

Menu

ORANGE-SPICED PRAWNS

CALIFORNIA FRITTATA

GINGER TUNA

ORIENTAL LAMB BROCHETTES with WATER CHESTNUTS

CHICKEN SONORA

ROASTED GARLIC and ALMOND CHEESE TART

FRESH CALIFORNIA FRUIT

SUGGESTED WINES: Begin with Champagne; then drink a
California Chardonnay or Pinot Noir.

Orange-spiced Prawns

MARINADE

2 cups frozen orange juice concentrate
1 cup peanut oil
1 cup soy sauce
½ cup dry white wine
½ cup Mendocino Mustard or any sweet hot mustard
1 tablespoon Asian sesame oil
1 tablespoon five-spice powder (available in Chinese markets)
4 garlic cloves

5½ pounds large prawns (18 to 20 prawns per pound), peeled
  and deveined

Put all the ingredients for the marinade in a blender and blend until well mixed. (You may have to do this in two batches.) Place the prawns in a glass or stainless steel bowl. Pour the marinade over the prawns, cover the bowl, and marinate in the refrigerator for 3 to 4 hours. Remove from the refrigerator 30 minutes before cooking. The prawns can be cooked under a broiler or grilled over charcoal for about 5 minutes. They are done as soon as they become opaque.

California Frittata

SERVES FIFTY

4 cups minced onions
4 tablespoons peanut oil
4 ears of corn
Two 7-ounce cans diced peeled green chilies
One 14-ounce can chopped black olives, drained
10 cooked artichoke hearts, chopped
3 cups shredded Tillamook cheese

1 cup grated Parmesan cheese
2 teaspoons Tabasco
½ teaspoon ground black pepper
2 dozen eggs, beaten

In a sauté pan, cook the onions in the oil until the onions are translucent. Set aside. Cut the kernels off of the ears of corn. Combine the corn and onions with all of the remaining ingredients and divide evenly into 2 oiled 9-by-13-inch casseroles. Place in a preheated 350° oven and bake for 30 to 40 minutes until well set. Let cool for 15 minutes and then cut into small wedges. This frittata can be served with fresh salsa and sour cream.

GINGER TUNA

SERVES FIFTY

MARINADE

½ cup peanut oil
½ cup *sake*
½ cup Westbrae Tofu Sauce (available in natural food stores)
½ cup Mendocino Mustard or any sweet hot mustard
2 teaspoons chopped fresh ginger
3 garlic cloves
½ teaspoon chili oil (available in Chinese markets)

4 pounds fresh tuna fillets, cut into 1-inch dice

Combine all of the ingredients for the marinade in a blender or food processor and mix until well blended. Place the tuna in a glass or stainless steel bowl and pour the marinade over it. Refrigerate for 2 hours. Remove from the refrigerator 30 minutes before cooking. Cook under the broiler for about 2 minutes, or until the fish is barely translucent at the center. Serve with wooden sandwich picks or skewers.

Oriental Lamb Brochettes with Water Chestnuts

SERVES FIFTY

The sesame-chili oil, five-spice powder, and Sechuan peppercorns are all found in Chinese markets.

MARINADE

1 tablespoon Sechuan peppercorns
½ cup Westbrae Tofu Sauce (available in natural food stores)
¼ cup soy sauce
½ cup dry sherry
2 tablespoons sesame-chili oil
3 tablespoons minced fresh garlic
3 tablespoons minced fresh ginger
1 tablespoon five-spice powder

6 pounds leg of lamb, cut into 1-inch dice
3 pounds fresh whole water chestnuts, peeled, or 3 pounds canned
   peeled whole water chestnuts, drained

To make the marinade, in a heavy skillet toast the peppercorns for 3 or 4 minutes. Then in a blender purée them for about 2 minutes. In a large container, add the peppercorns to all the other marinade ingredients and mix well. Add the lamb and toss well. Cover and marinate in the refrigerator for 3 or 4 hours. Add the water chestnuts for the last 30 minutes. Remove from the refrigerator 30 minutes before cooking. Thread the lamb and water chestnuts onto wooden skewers that have been soaked in water. Grill over an open charcoal fire until medium rare.

Chicken Sonora

SERVES FIFTY

MARINADE

½ cup Mexican tomato salsa
¼ cup peanut oil
¼ cup fresh lime juice
¼ cup Mendocino Mustard or any sweet hot mustard
2 fresh *tomatillos,* husks removed, or 2 whole canned *tomatillos**
2 teaspoons ground cumin
3 garlic cloves, minced
1 tablespoon chopped fresh cilantro

5 pounds boned skinned chicken breasts, cut into 1-by-2-inch strips
1 cup sesame seeds

Place all the ingredients for the marinade in a blender or food processor and purée until well mixed. Place the marinade in a large glass or stainless steel bowl with the chicken strips and marinate for 2 to 3 hours in the refrigerator. Take the chicken out of the marinade 30 minutes before cooking and dip it in the sesame seeds. Grill the chicken under a broiler or over charcoal until barely opaque.

* *Tomatillos,* or husk tomatoes, may be found in Latino markets and many large supermarkets.

Roasted Garlic and Almond Cheese Tart

SERVES FIFTY

4 tablespoons almonds
10 large garlic cloves
3 tablespoons peanut oil
1 pound ricotta cheese
2 tablespoons Mendocino Mustard or any sweet hot mustard
2 tablespoons chopped fresh chives
2 tablespoons minced shallots
3 eggs
1 pound cream cheese at room temperature
3 baked 9-inch pastry shells

Preheat the oven to 300°. Toast the almonds on a baking sheet for about 10 minutes, let cool, and then coarsely chop. In a baking pan, toss the garlic cloves in the peanut oil. Roast in the lower third of the oven until the garlic is soft and golden (approximately 35 to 40 minutes). Let cool 20 minutes. Place the garlic and oil in a blender or food processor and chop. And the cream cheese, ricotta, mustard, chives, and shallots and purée until blended and smooth (you may blend in the cream cheese after the mixture is removed from the blender if there is no room in your blender at this point). Add the eggs and blend until a smooth consistency is reached. Pour into the pastry shells and sprinkle the almonds over the top of the tarts. Bake at 350° for approximately 20 to 25 minutes or until the surfaces barely jiggle. Cool the tarts on a rack and serve at room temperature.

Van Wyk
Associates

Nancy Van Wyk heads a company that enjoys the challenge of producing special events on a large scale. Recently she mustered more than three hundred workers and 2½ tons of food for ten parties on Super Bowl Sunday, as well as catering for the Republican and Democratic national conventions. This sit-down dinner for sixty, created by chef Brian Leonard, can be presented in a large home or a rented location with a kitchen staff of three. The recipes may be cut in half or by a third to accommodate the number of guests invited.

• • • • •

MENU

PEPPERED FILET of BEEF with
SAFFRON MAYONNAISE

GRILLED SCALLOPS with BLACK FOREST HAM

STUFFED CHERRY TOMATOES

ARTICHOKE HEARTS and CRAYFISH with
SAUCE NANTUA

FRESHLY BAKED HERBED BREAD

GRILLED NOISETTES of LAMB with ROAST GARLIC

BRAISED LEEKS and CARROTS

SAUTEED LENTILS and SHALLOTS

ASSORTED SMALL PASTRIES:
Almond Florentines with Dark-Chocolate Strips,
Linzertorte Cookies, Vanilla Madeleines,
White Chocolate Truffles with Hazelnuts

SUGGESTED WINES: Serve a California Chardonnay with the artichoke hearts and crayfish; and a California Merlot or Zinfandel with the lamb.

Peppered Filet of Beef with Saffron Mayonnaise

MAKES 180 HOR D'OEUVRES

Cured and smoked peppered filet of beef is thinly sliced and presented on a crisp crouton with a rosette of freshly prepared saffron mayonaise.

15 garlic cloves, chopped
1 cup black peppercorns, crushed
¼ cup chopped fresh thyme
¼ cup chopped fresh oregano
¼ cup chopped fresh rosemary
1 cup sugar
1 cup sea salt
1 cup olive oil
One 5½-pound filet of beef, tied with string
4 baguettes
1 cup mayonnaise (preferably homemade)
Saffron to taste

Mix the garlic, black pepper, thyme, oregano, rosemary, sugar, sea salt, and olive oil in a bowl to form a paste. Place the filet in a container and completely cover with the paste mixture; let it marinate covered in the refrigerator 1 to 2 days.

Prepare a fire, using mesquite charcoal, in a covered grill. Once the fire has died and the coals are glowing, push the coals to both sides of the grill. Place an aluminum roasting pan in the center and fill it half full with water. Place one handful of hickory chips soaked in water or fresh fruit-tree cuttings over the coals. Replace the grill and place the filet over the drip pan. Cover and smoke 30 minutes for rare beef or 45 minutes for medium beef. When the filet is cooked, remove and refrigerate until it is cold.

Meanwhile, cut ¼-inch-thick slices from the baguettes and toast lightly on baking sheets in a 375° oven. Lightly mix the mayonnaise with saffron to taste. When the filet is cooled, remove the string and thinly slice. Loosely roll a slice of beef and place one on each crouton. With a pastry bag, pipe a rosette of mayonnaise on one end of the beef.

Grilled Scallops with Black Forest Ham

SERVES SIXTY

120 bay scallops (about 1 pound)
30 thin slices of Black Forest ham, cut in quarters

Take 2 scallops and wrap them with a quarter piece of Black Forest ham. Skewer with a toothpick. Repeat for all of the scallops. To cook, place on a open charcoal grill for about 90 seconds.

Stuffed Cherry Tomatoes

SERVES SIXTY

120 cherry tomatoes (about 4 baskets)
Salt to taste
1½ cups rice wine vinegar
1 cup water
2 pounds carrots, minced
1 medium cauliflower, minced
1 pound broccoli, minced
1 bunch green onions, minced
Salt and pepper to taste
Pinch of minced fresh dill

Cut off the top part of the cherry tomatoes. Scoop out the insides, lightly salt, and drain. Combine the vinegar and water with the vegetables and seasonings. Refrigerate for 6 hours. Drain the vegetables and stuff the tomatoes.

Artichoke Hearts and Crayfish with Sauce Nantua

SERVES SIXTY

60 medium artichokes
25 pounds live crayfish

SAUCE

½ cup butter
1 pound carrots, chopped
1 bunch celery, chopped
2 onions, chopped
Reserved crayfish shells
1½ gallons water
1½ quarts heavy cream

21 leeks, white part only, cut in julienne
10 cucumbers, peeled and seeded
Salt and cayenne to taste
17 bunches *mâche* (lamb's lettuce)
Zest of 10 lemons, cut into strips
Cracked black pepper to taste

Cut all the leaves from the artichokes. Using a paring knife, remove the chokes and rub fresh lemon juice on the hearts to keep them from oxidizing. Blanch the hearts in salted water until *al dente,* about 20 minutes, and then chill. Poach the crayfish in salted water for 5 to 7 minutes. Peel and devein them and reserve the shells for the sauce. Chill the crayfish.

To make the sauce, melt the butter in a stockpot and sauté the vegetables for about 5 minutes; add the reserved shells and sauté a few minutes longer. Add the water and reduce by one-third. Remove the shells with a slotted spoon and mash them in a mortar, blender, or food processor. Return the shells to the sauce. Reduce the sauce by one-half. Strain through a fine sieve (if necessary, then strain through cheesecloth). Return the sauce to the heat and add the cream. Bring the sauce to a boil, immediately remove it, and chill.

Mix the crayfish, leeks, and cucumbers together with enough sauce to moisten. Season with salt and cayenne.

Pour ¼ cup of sauce on each salad plate. Place a portion of *mâche* at the 12 o'clock position. Place the artichoke bottom at the base of the *mâche* and fill with the crayfish mixture. Garnish with lemon zest and cracked black pepper.

Grilled Noisettes of Lamb with Roast Garlic

SERVES SIXTY

20 racks of lamb
2 pounds carrots, minced
2 pounds celery, minced
2 pounds onions, minced
Garlic cloves from 1 head of garlic
1 cup tomato paste
2 bay leaves
1 pound peppercorns
2 bottles Merlot wine
30 heads of garlic, outer papery layers removed
Olive oil
1 cup butter
1 pound shallots, chopped
Salt and pepper to taste

The day before, debone the racks of lamb. In a shallow baking pan, roast the bones in a 450° oven until brown. Add the carrots, celery, onion, and garlic to the pan. Spread the tomato paste over the bones, return them to the oven, and cook until the tomato paste is lightly burned (this produces a rich color for the stock). Remove the bones and place in a stockpot. Cover with cold water and add the bay leaves and peppercorns. Deglaze the pan with 1 bottle of Merlot and add this to the bones. Simmer and reduce uncovered on very low heat for 5 to 6 hours. *continued*

The next day, prepare the lamb. Remove the nerve from the bottom of the lamb pieces. Remove all fat and silver skin from the filet portion. Be careful not to separate the filet from the flap of meat and skin that ran up the rack of bones. When cleaned, lightly cross-score the flap and pound lightly with a meat cleaver. Wrap the flap around the meat to cover and cut the excess off. Tie with cotton string at each end and at ½-inch intervals. Slice between the strings to make *noisettes* ½ inch thick. One rack should yield 9 pieces or 3 portions.

Strain the stock and simmer uncovered until the yield is approximately 1 gallon. Meanwhile, brush the heads of garlic with olive oil. Place them in a roasting pan in a 200° oven for about 1½ hours or until soft to the touch. Quarter the heads and keep them warm.

Melt ½ cup of the butter in a stockpot. Sauté the shallots until translucent, then add the second bottle of Merlot. Simmer uncovered until it is reduced to a syrupy glaze. Add the stock and season with salt and pepper. Just before serving, whisk in the remaining ½ cup of butter a bit at a time. This will soften the acidity of the wine and give the sauce a nice lustre.

Salt and pepper the *noisettes* and grill over mesquite charcoal on an open grill. Remove from the fire and cut the string to serve. Serve each person 3 *noisettes* of lamb with ¼ cup of sauce and 1 roast garlic clove.

BRAISED LEEKS AND CARROTS

SERVES SIXTY

1 pound butter
8 pounds baby carrots
9 pounds baby leeks
3 cups water
Salt and pepper to taste

Melt the butter in a sauté pan and add the carrots. Sauté over low heat for 5 minutes, then add the leeks, water, and salt and pepper. Cover and simmer until tender.

Sautéed Lentils and Shallots

9 pounds lentils, soaked in water to cover overnight
1½ pounds shallots, chopped
1 cup butter
Salt and pepper to taste

Drain the lentils and simmer them in salted water to cover until tender, about 30 minutes. Drain. Melt the butter in a sauté pan and sauté the shallots until translucent. Add the lentils and sauté until heated through. Add salt and pepper to taste.

COCOLAT

*A*lice Medrich is the founder and owner of Cocolat, the birthplace of the American chocolate truffle in the 1970s. Much larger than its European counterpart, this extraordinary confection touched off the chocolate truffle revolution that has spread across the country.

Alice created Schön Rosmarin especially for the San Francisco String Quartet. The dessert is elegant but playful—a delightful accompaniment to Fritz Kreisler's "Schön Rosmarin" on the musical cassette. Alice introduces her recipe as follows:

"Schön Rosmarin is a frivolous but elegant dessert with delightful contrasts: light crisp coffee meringues with cold creamy ice cream, fresh tangy fruits, smooth whipped cream and chocolate sauce! Schmaltzy? Yes—and simple to make, since most parts may be made in advance."

•   •   •   •   •

Schön Rosmarin

SERVES TEN TO TWELVE

MERINGUE LAYERS

3 egg whites at room temperature
⅛ teaspoon cream of tartar
2 teaspoons instant espresso powder
¾ cup sugar

1 pint premium vanilla ice cream
1½ cups heavy cream
1 teaspoon vanilla extract
1 tablespoon sugar, or to taste
1 basket fresh strawberries or raspberries, or 1½ cups sliced kiwis or
　other favorite fruits
Chocolate Sauce, following

To make the meringue layers, preheat the oven to 250°. Combine the egg whites, cream of tartar, and coffee powder in a clean, dry mixer bowl. Beat until soft peaks form, then slowly sprinkle in the sugar, continuing to beat until the meringue is very stiff.

Cover a cookie sheet with a piece of parchment paper. Trace two 8-inch circles on the parchment. Scrape the meringue into a pastry bag fitted with a decorative tip and pipe a swirly decorative ring of meringue around the inside of both of the traced circles. With the remaining meringue completely fill in each of the circles so that you have 2 meringue layers with decorative edges (the centers won't show).

Bake for 2 hours or more, until the meringue layers are perfectly light, dry, and crisp. If possible, allow them to cool in a turned-off oven with the door closed. Wrap the cooled meringues airtight in plastic wrap until needed.

Soften the ice cream for 30 to 45 minutes in the refrigerator until it can be spooned out easily but is not too mushy.

Place 1 coffee meringue layer on a serving platter and begin spooning softened ice cream over the meringue up to about 1 inch from the edge of the meringue layer. Use all of the ice cream and compact it gently (don't break the meringue!) and smooth the top surface with a warmed spatula if necessary. Place the second layer of meringue firmly over the ice cream and center it. (It will overhang the ice cream by about 1 inch.) Wrap the entire dessert in plastic wrap and freeze hard until 45 to 60 minutes before serving. (This may be done several days in advance for convenience.)

About an hour before serving, whip the cream with the vanilla and sugar. Scrape into a pastry bag fitted with the same tip used to pipe the meringue. Pipe swirls of cream around the dessert between the meringue layers, completely hiding the ice cream layer. Pipe a ring of swirls on top of the dessert about an inch from the outer edge and fill in the center of the circle with more cream. Place whole or sliced fruit on top in the circle of cream.

Rewarm the chocolate sauce, if necessary, before presenting the dessert at the table. Pass the sauce separately and allow each guest to help him or herself.

CHOCOLATE SAUCE

MAKES ABOUT 1½ CUPS

10 ounces semisweet or bittersweet chocolate, cut or broken into
small pieces
⅓ cup milk
½ teaspoon vanilla extract

Combine the chocolate and milk in a double boiler and melt over barely simmering water, stirring frequently until smooth. Off the heat add the vanilla and stir in. Use the warm sauce immediately or set aside until needed and reheat briefly.

A time-honored recipe and an old-fashioned belief in quality laid the foundation for Just Desserts in 1974, when an enterprising young couple began baking cheesecakes in their home kitchen. Joined by two partners, the foursome has established four retail stores and an ever expanding wholesale business in the San Francisco Bay Area. Just Desserts makes all of its desserts from scratch and bakes them to order daily. The recipe for Rondeau was created at Just Desserts by Jane Fay.

• • • • •

RONDEAU

SERVES EIGHT TO TWELVE

Although this recipe has quite a few steps, it is relatively quick and easy to make if you assemble all the ingredients and tools before you begin. The cake and filling can be made the day before and frosted the next morning.

FILLING

¼ cup Grand Marnier
1½ teaspoons plain gelatin
½ cup powdered sugar
Grated zest of 1 large orange
1 cup chilled heavy cream

CAKE

1½ ounces (1½ squares) unsweetened chocolate
⅔ cup butter, cut into 4 or 5 pieces and chilled
½ cup sugar
4 eggs, separated
1 teaspoon vanilla extract
⅔ cup sifted cake flour
1 tablespoon cornstarch

Powdered sugar

GLAZE

7 tablespoons superfine sugar
⅓ cup fresh-brewed coffee
½ ounce (½ square) semisweet chocolate
1 tablespoon corn syrup
1 tablespoon butter
2 tablespoons Kahlúa

To make the filling, put the Grand Marnier in the top of a double boiler. Sprinkle the gelatin evenly over the surface, but do not get any on the sides of the pan. Allow the gelatin to absorb all the liquid (10 to 15 minutes), then put it over boiling water and gently stir until it is completely dissolved. (Test by rubbing some liquid between your fingers; there should be no granules.) Allow this to cool to room temperature. Mix the sugar and orange zest together. Whip the cream and add the sugar-zest mixture in 4 to 5 batches. Whip the cream to soft peaks; do not overwhip because the cream will go flat. Whisk in the Grand Marnier. Stop immediately and scrape any Grand Marnier off the side of the bowl. If it has hardened, remove it. Do not mix it in. Continue to mix until the peaks come back. Refrigerate for an hour or so before using.

To make the cake, preheat the oven to 400 °. Butter a jelly roll pan and line it with waxed paper that has been buttered and lightly floured. Shake off any excess flour.

Melt the chocolate in a double boiler over low heat. Set it aside in the double boiler. Cream the butter and half of the sugar together until the mixture is light and fluffy or until you can barely feel the sugar granules when you rub the mixture between your thumb and forefinger. Scrape and mix for a minute or so. Add one yolk at a time. (Wait until you can't see any more yolk in the mix before adding the next one.) Scrape thoroughly and mix well. Repeat this with the remaining yolks. Add the vanilla. Before adding the melted chocolate, be sure it is not too hot by checking it with your finger. If it is no warmer than your finger, it is the right temperature. Add the melted chocolate. Scrape and mix until well blended. Sift the four and cornstarch together and fold in. Cut and fold until it is fully incorporated. Do not stir, as you will stir all the air out.

Whisk the egg whites at medium speed in a clean bowl. Be sure no fat or oil is in the bowl or your whites will not whip. Continue until you see more white than yellow. At this point begin to add the remaining ¼ cup of sugar a little at a time (around 5 additions). Beat until you have firm peaks and the mix is shiny. Take one-third or so of the whipped whites and fold into the cake mixture. Cut and fold in completely. Repeat using one-third of the whites, and repeat with the last third. Gently spread evenly in the prepared pan. Put the pan on the middle oven shelf. Bake for 5 minutes or until a cake tester comes out clean.

continued

While the cake is baking, dust a clean kitchen towel generously with sifted powdered sugar. When the cake is done, remove it from the oven and immediately turn it out onto the sugared towel (if you have any trouble, take hold of the edges and gently shake to loosen it). Peel off the paper and trim any crisp edges. Roll the cake up in the towel lengthwise and let it rest for a minute. Unroll it and let it rest for 2 to 3 minutes. Roll it back up in the towel and let it cool completely.

Carefully unroll the cake and fill it evenly with the Grand Marnier filling. Re-roll and place seam side down. At this point you can wrap the cake in aluminum foil and store it overnight.

To make the glaze, heat the sugar and coffee together over low heat, stirring until the sugar is dissolved. Be careful—do not burn the coffee. Add the chocolate and corn syrup. Heat to boiling, stirring constantly. Cook at slow rolling boil for 4 minutes or until you see bubbles forming a half inch from the side of the pot. Remove from the heat and stir in the butter and the Kahlúa. Beat the glaze until it thickens. A good gauge is to feel the bottom of the bowl: if it is still slightly warm, it's done. Immediately pour the glaze down the center of the log and use your fingers to spread it evenly on the sides. Refrigerate for at least 1 hour. Decorate as the occasion requires.

LA VIENNOISE

*K*aren Shapiro has been a pastry chef for fourteen years. She founded La Viennoise in 1978 with a desire for the independence to produce her own pastry creations. The traditional Viennese Linzertorte she presents here will be perfectly accompanied by the compositions of the Viennese composers Lehár, Kreisler, and Strauss on the musical cassette.

· · · · ·

Linzertorte

1 cup salted butter at room temperature, cut into chunks
1½ cups ground unblanched almonds
1 cup sugar
1 teaspoon vanilla extract
1 egg
2¼ cups unbleached all-purpose flour
1 cup raspberry jam
1 egg mixed with
2 teaspoons milk or half and half

Place the butter in a mixer along with the ground almonds and sugar. Mix to blend with a paddle attachment; when blended, add the vanilla and egg and continue mixing to a thick paste. Add the flour last and mix until blended to a soft dough. If you are not using a mixer, mix the flour, sugar, and nuts in a bowl. Cut or blend in the butter, then the egg and vanilla. Mix to a paste. Chill the dough until firm.

Preheat the oven to 350°. Divide the dough into 2 uneven parts—roughly two-thirds and one-third. Roll out the larger portion to a circle slightly larger than the pan and ⅜ inch thick. Line an 8-inch round springform cake pan with the dough, trimming the sides to a height of about ½ to ¾ inch. Spread the jam evenly on top of the dough. Roll out the remaining dough (again ⅜-inch thick) in a rectangle. Cut into ⅜-inch-wide strips. Lay the strips evenly onto the jam, parallel to one another, about ¾ inch apart. Brush the lattice strips with egg wash. Lay another set of strips on top of the first set diagonally to make a diamond-shaped lattice. Brush these strips with egg wash. To finish the edge with a border, lay additional strips around the edge (touching the pan), then egg wash this. Chill the assembled torte. Bake for 40 to 50 minutes or until golden brown—the jam will begin to bubble. Cool before removing from the pan.

Sheraton-Palace Hotel

THE GARDEN COURT

T he Garden Court of San Francisco's Sheraton-Palace Hotel was rebuilt from the Grand Court of the old Palace Hotel after the Earthquake and Fire of 1906. It has been called "the most beautiful dining room in the world." The leaded glass dome that covers the expanse of the room, the splendid Italian marble columns, and the brilliant chandeliers evoke the feeling of old San Francisco and are an architectural reminder of the warmth and depth of San Francisco's heritage.

A finale to dinner in the Garden Court is the popular and traditional trifle bowl. I have seen this trifle enjoyed by thousands of guests of the Garden Court while our string quartet has been in residence there for the past ten years. This Victorian dessert is an example of San Francisco's historical cuisine that is still bringing enjoyment today. Serve this perfect party dessert in your most beautiful glass bowl.

• • • • •

GARDEN COURT TRIFLE BOWL

SERVES EIGHT TO TEN

PASTRY CREAM

3 cups milk
½ cup butter
⅔ cup sugar
1 tablespoon vanilla extract
10 eggs, beaten
½ cup cornstarch

SPONGE CAKE

10 eggs
1 cup sugar
½ cup melted butter
1 cup cake flour

4 cups heavy cream
One 10-ounce package frozen raspberries, thawed, or 1 cup canned
  raspberry sauce
2 cups fruit cocktail or mixed fresh fruit: sliced strawberries, cherries,
  peaches, pears, etc.
½ cup sweet sherry

To make the pastry cream, bring the milk, butter, sugar, and vanilla to
a boil in the top of a double boiler and then remove from the heat. Mix
the eggs and cornstarch together and gradually add this to the double
boiler, stirring constantly until thick and creamy. Do not allow to boil.
Set aside to cool.

To make the cake, preheat the oven to 375°. Mix the eggs, sugar,
and butter together with an electric mixer for 10 minutes. Sprinkle the
flour over the egg mixture ¼ cup at a time and fold it in carefully.
Pour the batter into 2 buttered and floured 10-inch round pans. Bake
for 15 to 20 minutes. Let the sponge cake cool completely in the pans,
set on racks.

Whip the cream until it has soft peaks. Purée the frozen raspberries in a blender or food processor. Mix the purée with the fruit and sherry. Remove the sponge cakes from the pans and place 1 cake on the bottom of a large glass bowl. Pour over the cake half of the pastry cream, then half of the fruit mixture, then half of the whipped cream. Place the second cake on top of this and repeat the layering in the same order. You may garnish the top layer of whipped cream with cherries or other fruits.

INDEX

Sharon O'Connor, cellist and founder of the San Francisco String Quartet, grew up cooking and playing music in California. She has been performing with the San Francisco String Quartet for more than ten years.